THE JOHN TRAVOLTA
ANNUAL 1980

CONTENTS

Published in Great Britain by Stafford Pemberton Publishing Ltd.,
The Ruskin Chambers, Drury Lane, Knutsford, Cheshire WA16 6HA.

JOHN TRAVOLTA'S
Lifelines

Personal side of a Superstar

Real name: John Joseph Travolta
Date of Birth: 18th February 1954
Starsign: Aquarius
Birthplace: Englewood, New Jersey, USA
Parents' names: Salvatore (Sam) and Helen
Brothers and sisters: two older brothers Joey and Sam Jnr, and three older sisters, Ellen, Margaret and Ann.
Height: 6ft. 0ins.
Weight: around 170lbs.
Colour of hair: very dark brown
Colour of eyes: blue
Education: Dwight Morrow Public High School, Englewood
First public appearance: in 'Who'll Kill The Ploughboy?' at The New Dimension Theatre, Englewood (aged 12)
Nickname: (as a child) 'Bone' (because he was very thin)
Religion: Scientology
Favourite singer: Barbra Streisand
Favourite actors: Marlon Brando, Robert De Niro
Favourite clothes: T-shirts and jeans, denim workshirts and baggy cardigans
Favourite food: no special favourite, but has always had a sweet tooth
Personality: intelligent, reserved, courteous and unselfish, tends to be more of an introvert than an extrovert.
Ambition: To remain popular by always keeping one step ahead of his public and keeping a few surprises up his sleeve.

JOHN'S IDEAL GIRL

JOHN TRAVOLTA is one of the most attractive bachelor prospects in the world, but did you ever stop to think what kind of steady girlfriend he'd want if he decided to start a romance?

Unlike his screen image as the brash disco king or the cocky college boy, the real John Travolta is more introverted.

As an Aquarian he's quiet, sincere and cares for others, so the lucky woman would most likely have been shy herself when she first met John. At the same time, Aquarians love being busy and travelling, so she'd have a desire to see new places and take an active interest in John's marvellous career.

Talking about travelling, she'd probably have to get used to doing most of that in the passenger seat of John's private plane. Flying is one of John's main hobbies, just ahead of fast cars and fast motorbikes, and he's pretty good at it too.

Who knows? – if his acting career hadn't taken off so dramatically, he might have ended up as a pilot. He wouldn't be too happy if his companion kept remembering other appointments every time John mentioned the hangars and a weekend holiday by plane.

She wouldn't try to make sure that John always wore a three-piece suit in public. He likes to dress in shorts and beach shoes if the sun is out or in jeans and a T-shirt if it isn't – but whatever the weather, he likes to feel relaxed in his clothes.

Of course, this makes some people think that John doesn't care about his appearance. Nothing could be further from the truth. Because John looks pretty neat himself, even casual clothes on him have a habit of looking well-chosen and elegant.

She'd have to realise just how important John's career is to him. When he gets engrossed in his work, he devotes his full attention to giving a totally professional performance. He doesn't take kindly to periods of inactivity – although there aren't too many of them any more – and he wouldn't like trivial interruptions when his mind is getting 'geared up' to deliver another performance of a lifetime.

But taking an interest in John's career wouldn't be one of the harder 'conditions', would it?

She'd have another advantage if she enjoyed watching the occasional game of tennis or basketball. 'Showbiz' is the main characteristic of Travolta, but love of sports runs pretty deep as well. Like any other outdoor hobby John tries, he runs the risk of attracting a large audience every time he takes the field – and they're not always content just to watch from the sidelines! – but there's still nothing that he likes more than the sight of a basketball net at close range.

That would be quite a girl – modest, sincere but energetic, keen on flying, fast cars and sport, and eager to play more than a bit part in developing the career of one of the screen's biggest stars.

But then she'd be getting quite a guy as well!

The early years

HOW JT MADE HIS FIRST STEPS ON THE ROAD TO SUPERSTARDOM

JOHN JOSEPH Travolta was born on the 18th February 1954 in the town of Englewood, New Jersey, about a half-hour's drive out of New York city. He is the youngest of six children, three boys and three girls, all of whom have grown up to be involved in show business in some way.

The Travolta brothers and sisters inherited their love of music and drama from their mother Helen, a fine actress who had also, in the Thirties, been a member of a radio vocal group called 'The Sunshine Sisters'. By the time that John was born she had largely given up acting herself in favour of teaching drama and staging numerous productions in the locality.

From his father Salvatore, known to one and all as Sam, John inherited his athleticism. Sam had in his day been a highly talented football player and it is from him that John got his love of sports, particularly basketball at which he excelled at school.

But acting and music were the main things and they attracted John from a very early age. The family remember him well cavorting about in front on the television mimicking Jimmy Ganey, his hero of the time, doing 'Yankee Doodle Dandy'. John watched, green with envy, while his elder brothers and sisters landed themselves parts in various professional and amateur productions and pestered his mother

relentlessly for a chance to be in something himself.

She felt he had talent and was keen to encourage him and, by the time he was 12, he had played bit parts in two local productions.

The first real money he earned from acting was when, at 16, he landed a role in a production of the musical 'Bye Bye Birdie' during the school holidays for the princely sum of 50 dollars a week.

After that he was badly bitten by the theatrical bug and pleaded with his parents to allow him to leave school. His father was reluctant to allow him to do so as his end of year grades had been far from good, but eventually he relented. He did, however, impose one condition – that if young John had failed to make any headway as an actor after a year, he would return to his studies.

John himself had already decided that if things did not work out for him as an actor, he would train to become a pilot instead. He had always been almost as crazy about aeroplanes as he had about the theatre.

Fortunately for John, he did well enough in his first year out of school not to have to honour his promise to his father. The breaks came and gradually he was on his way to becoming the world-wide superstar he is today. But he has always remained close to his family. Sadly his mother died in

December 1978 but his father still lives in Englewood and John goes to visit there as often as possible, although he has to sneak into town very quietly. There only has to be a whisper of a rumour go around that he has arrived and the house is besieged by fans wanting to catch a glimpse of him. Some of them have even been known to cut slivers of wood from the porch to take away as souvenirs.

When he is filming, John likes to have at least one member of his family along with him as moral support. He managed to land minor roles for his mother and his sister Ann in 'Saturday Night Fever' and his sister Ellen played the part of a waitress in 'Grease'.

There is no doubt that John had a very happy childhood, growing up in a family where encouragement was doled out more often than discipline, and home in Englewood is still one of the places that John Travolta most likes to be.

GREASE

THE MOVIE SENSATION THAT JOHN NEARLY TURNED DOWN

IN THE wake of the phenomenal success of 'Grease' it seems odd to imagine that the film at one time never looked like being made at all.

The producers of the film, Robert Stigwood, head of RSO (Robert Stigwood Organisation) the multi-faceted entertainment organisation, and Allan Carr, were both deeply convinced that the musical which had been such a big hit in theatres all over the world would translate into a successful movie. But the big film companies did not agree.

Their executives thought that the story, about a Fifties greaser and a goody-goody girl, would seem too dated and fail to attract today's teenagers into the cinema. But in the end through persistent persuasion Stigwood and Carr managed to pass their enthusiasm for the film project on to others and a film version of 'Grease' became a definite proposition.

Initially, Allan Carr hoped for the now late Elvis Presley and Ann-Margret to fill the lead roles. Then later he set his sights on getting Henry Winkler (The Fonz) to play Danny Zuko and a girl named Susan Dey, who had appeared in 'The Partridge Family,' to play Sandra Dee.

But that plan fell flat when Henry Winkler turned the role down. He had already, in 'Happy Days' played a Fifties character not far removed from Danny Zuko and he had had enough of it. To take on the role of Danny, he felt, would be to risk being typecast in that kind of role for good.

Shortly after Henry Winkler had turned down the role, Allan Carr saw John Travolta in 'Welcome Back Kotter' and felt that he would be ideal for the lead role in 'Grease'. Robert Stigwood agreed and promptly signed John to a three-picture deal. The first movie would be 'Saturday Night Fever', the second 'Grease' with something totally different to be the third.

The idea was that 'Saturday Night Fever' would be a vehicle to bring John to the attention of the public and then, once his name was established, 'Grease' would be the really big one. In the event, 'Saturday Night Fever' did its job beyond the wildest dreams of its makers and turned into such a monster success that there were fears that people might find 'Grease' something of an anti-climax after it. Happily that was not to be.

Work on 'Grease' began shortly after work on 'Saturday Night Fever' was completed and nobody yet realised what a hot property they had in the can with 'Saturday Night Fever'.

John Travolta certainly never imagined how big the film might be and just before shooting was due to start on 'Grease', he threw everyone associated with the film into a blind panic. He told them simply that he didn't want to do it. He had played a street punk in the long-running TV series 'Welcome Back Kotter', he reasoned, and now he had just played another in 'Saturday Night Fever'.

The character in 'Grease' might be from a different era but he was still just another teenage punk and wasn't three of them in a row just too many? Like Henry Winkler, John was beginning to get nervous about type-casting.

Fortunately, he was persuaded to change his mind. He was reminded that the third film of his contract would star him in a completely different role. Also, John figured, light musicals don't crop up that often and it might be a good while before he got offered another, so it was worth having a stab at after all.

Having changed his mind, he threw the whole of his energies into the project and everyone breathed again. But it had been a close thing.

JOHN ADORES KIDS

John Travolta, the most eligible bachelor in the world and the biggest Superstar of the Seventies, adores kids.

But hold on a minute! Before you conjure up a picture of John as a family man with a little Travolta on each knee – and that's quite a picture – remember that this is a maybe for the future.

Right now, as his cinema career takes him from one hit film to another, he simply hasn't got the time to settle down and become the head of his own family.

On those few occasions when he can duck the limelight and spend a quiet evening with friends, the children on his knee belong to someone else. For one thing, his career has given him a reputation for doing things properly, and marriage in John's book would deserve just the same 100 per cent thought and dedication as his work.

Even John Travolta hasn't got 200 per cent. Also, he still feels that he owes a debt to the fans who put him where he is today. A private family life could take him away from his public, and he is the sort of guy who would consider something like that too. Some stars have enjoyed their success and fame but then gone on to ignore their public

John knows that's wrong. That's why he always finds time to say 'hello' and sign an autograph – unless a few more people in the queue begin a stampede – and that's why he still keeps his earliest newspaper interviews and front covers, reminding him of the way it all began.

If the gossip columnists had their way, John would be getting married once a week. He knows that he can't visit a restaurant

or film premiere accompanied by a girl without providing the gossip columns with desperately needed ammunition.

But there's no way such talk will influence John. He has a very determined personality.

He's in control of his life on the romantic front just as much as he's in control when the film cameras are rolling. He's observed his friends and peers in the acting profession and hasn't become too big-headed to notice the most sensible way of organising his career. John wants to know all about a film before he commits himself, however much money the producer offers him.

He knows he's probably right for the part, but is the part right for him? In his film, 'Minute By Minute,' he unveils a new facet of his acting talent – and this from a guy still in his twenties who's already proved that he can act, dance, sing and even turn on a bit of comedy. We'll be seeing a more serious side of John in a film about a man's relationship with an older woman, and maybe a personal side will be on view as well.

Remember that John's one lasting relationship was with Diana Hyland, an actress seventeen years his senior.

And as long as he cares for his fans that much, he won't be in any hurry to make Salvatore a proud grandfather. He's still the most eligible bachelor in the world!

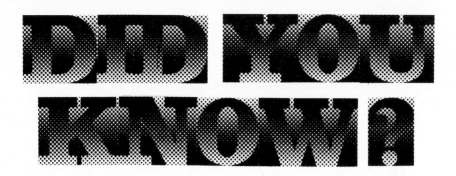

DID YOU KNOW?

DID YOU KNOW that the music the Bee Gees wrote for 'Saturday Night Fever' was composed in under a fortnight and without the group knowing more than the barest outline of the film's story. The group were in Paris when impresario Robert Stigwood approached them and told them he wanted them to write some music for the film.

He did not bother to fill them in on the whole story of the picture but he was very explicit about the music he required. For example, he told them that for one song, he wanted three sections of music of so many minutes each. Raw excitement to begin with, then a change of mood for the second section and a third to take the excitement way over the top.

The song which they delivered to him fitted his time requirements to the second and his mood requirements to perfection. They called it 'Stayin Alive'.

DID YOU KNOW that John Travolta caused quite an uproar during a trip to England last year when he turned down a request for a photographic session from Lord Snowdon, former husband of Princess Margaret?

Most actors would give their eye-teeth to be photographed by Lord Snowdon and many people thought that John was getting too big for his boots when he turned the request down, but John unperturbed explained: "I'm not English, I'm American and I don't know anything much about Lord Snowdon or his work and generally I prefer to work with photographers whose pictures are known to me."

DID YOU KNOW that John Travolta is sometimes accused of being a real old scruff? The reason is that he is sometimes spotted in public wearing two or three days growth of stubble on his chin. It's not that he can not be bothered to look his best when he goes out, but he has a sensitive skin which tends to break out in a rash if subjected to the razor too often.

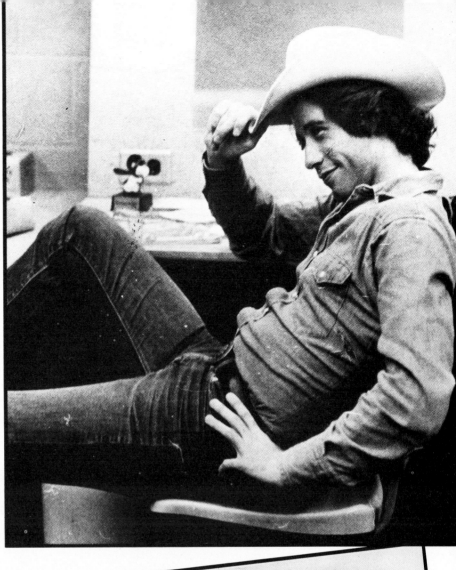

DID YOU KNOW that John Travolta has a jet aircraft which he is never allowed to pilot and another plane which he can only fly when he is not filming?

John has got a pilot's licence to fly single-engined aircraft and as one of his two planes is single-engined. He can fly that — but only when he is not filming. The company which insures him will only do so if, while his is shooting a film, he stays well away from his private aeroplane.

His other aircraft is a jet with more than one engine and since John is not qualified to pilot it, he has to content himself with travelling in it as a passenger.

JOHN AND THE FANS

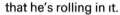

One person who just can't get to like John Travolta is his poor postman.

Every day he has to push about 1000 fan letters through John's letter box, and those letters cover every topic you can think of. One popular subject, of course, is the effect John has on his female followers. If he were to keep all the dates he gets invited to, he'd never find time for eating and sleeping, let alone acting.

Even reading his mail could take a sizeable chunk out of his busy day, but John likes to keep in touch with what his fans are feeling and he therefore reads as many as he can. Another

thing you have to learn to live with when you're a star of John Travolta's stature is the small percentage of letter-writing experts who specialise in envy.

Most of the boys think he's just as great as the girls do, but there's always the boyfriend who doesn't like the fact that his girl thinks about John rather too much!

For one thing, they want to know where he packs away all his money. John doesn't deny that he could be a proper dollar millionaire in the future, but he likes to dispel the impression

that he's rolling in it.

When a newspaper columnist announces the latest Travolta salary for a film, there's a big difference between that nice round figure and what eventually finds its way into John's bank account.

A star like John can't avoid having a retinue of staff, each with a particular job to do. He has business managers, a manager, an agent, all of whom operate on a set percentage of what John earns. Once he's paid them all, he still has to face the tax man.

There's always some hanger-on who expects John to pick up the tab in all the restaurants, and there's always the shop or business who'll add a few quick noughts onto his bills just because he's John Travolta.

It's the same for any star or personality but the problem increases along with fame – and John's pretty famous right now.

But this handful are the fans who don't really understand John or the necessary trappings of his career. Maybe one fan who ought to know is the legendary Fred Astaire, no stranger to the quick screen dance step himself.

Fred is often asked what he thinks of John, and he can't find anything but praise – not only for his acting and singing ability, but for his dancing, and Fred should know.

There is a place for sour grapes – but it's not John Travolta's letterbox. His true fans know that he is the greatest, and that he deserves every success which has come his way.

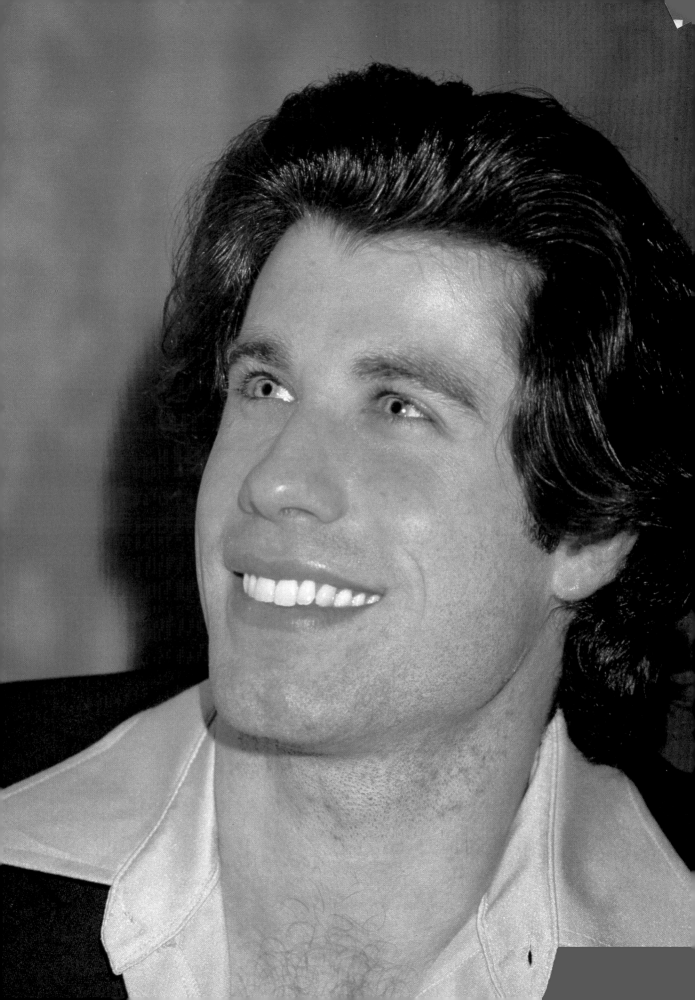

2001 Odyssey

– THE DISCO WHERE THE WORLD CAUGHT DISCO FEVER

WHILE JOHN Travolta was working on the character of Tony Manero, before filming of 'Saturday Night Fever' began, he quickly came to an important decision about the physical demands of the role.

"If this guy is supposed to be the best disco dancer," he told the film's director John Badham, "then I have to be the best disco dancer too." And with that aim in mind, he disappeared off into training.

He hired the man who trained Sylvester Stallone for the gruelling fight scenes in 'Rocky' to help him build up his own physical fitness with miles of running and weeks of punishing work-outs in the gymnasium.

At the end of it all, there was not a pound of flesh on his body that had not been turned into firm, rippling muscle to give him the stamina he would need for the tortuous routines he would be performing on film.

While John was away getting himself into shape to become the best disco dancer anyone had ever seen, the film's location expert was out looking for realism as well. He knew that the disco scenes would never look right performed in a mock-up film set, the disco had to be the real thing. To find the right setting for the disco fever, he went all over New York looking for the right place. Eventually, he settled on a disco called '2001 Odyssey,' the biggest in Brooklyn.

The place was convenient for housing a film crew, it had a dance floor that could accommodate about 50 dancers in comfort and, above all, it looked right. But even so, the film makers decided to put in a few extra touches of their own.

One 'touch' they wanted was to install a dance floor that lit up. This they did at a cost of a cool $20,000. They also installed a dry ice machine to create misty effects around the dancers, a mirror ball above the dance floor and other extra lighting effects. Then, finally, the walls were lined with shiny paper in bright colours and the disco for the film was ready.

So were the local fans, who had to hear that John Travolta would be filming at their disco. On the first day of actual filming, 4,000 of them turned up. Some of them even rocked the caravan John was using as a dressing room in the hope that, if he was inside it, he would come out! Some of the local regulars at the disco managed to get into the film as extras and to meet John himself.

They were surprised to find that the guy who was soon to start a whole new disco craze was not brash at all, but rather shy and unassuming. About one thing one and all of them were agreed. They liked him.

J.T. A-Z

A is for athletic, something John had to be to undertake the strenuous disco routines of 'Saturday Night Fever'. Luckily, he was already a good sportsman, especially playing basketball, but still he ran miles every day and did gymnasium workouts to get into peak condition.

B is for Barbarino – Vinnie Barbarino – the character who first made John Travolta a household name across America in the TV series 'Welcome Back Kotter'.

C is for Charisma, need we say more?

D is for discos and dancing, which have both enjoyed a boom across continents. And it all began with John Travolta.

E is for Englewood, the town in New Jersey where John was born.

f is for Fever. Travolta Fever is something the whole world has caught.

G is for Girls. According to the gossip columnist John is supposed to love a different one every day, but in truth he is a one woman man, who has not found love again since the tragic death two years ago of his girl friend Diana Hyland.

h is for Henry – Henry Winkler the Fonz. He and John Travolta, rivalling attractions in TV series, are supposed to be deadly enemies, but really they are the best of friends.

i is for Inspiration, something John has been to every disco fanatic the world over.

J is for John and Joseph, both of Travolta's first names.

K is for Kotter, the lead character in the TV series which launched John as a star.

L is for Luck. John's had his fair share of lucky breaks in his career but there have been low moments too.

m is for musicals like 'Grease' and 'Saturday Night Fever', which have earned John his huge following across the world.

N is for nostalgia. 'Grease' is a nostalgic look at the 1950s but made fresh and alive by the brilliance of the music and the acting.

 is for Olivia, John's beautiful co-star in 'Grease'.

P is for Personality, something that really shines through on John's records and in his acting.

Q is for quizzes. Try your hand at the John Travolta superquiz in this annual.

 is for Robert Stigwood, the show-business impresario who signed John Travolta to a three-picture film contract.

S is for Staturday, best night of the week for disco mania.

T is for Travolta, the man of the moment.

 is for us, the people who buy the records and see the films. We're not such a bad lot really!

is for Versatility. Something John has shown in his brilliant abilities to act, sing and dance.

 is for Work and the long hours of it John put in on his films, shows that being a film star isn't all glamour.

 is for X-certificate, which meant that some people had to wait until they were old enough to see 'Saturday Night Fever' legally.

is for Yachts, the status symbol often associated with the rich and famous. But John doesn't have one. He prefers faster transport like powerful cars, motorbikes and, of course, aeroplanes.

is for Zuko – Danny Zuko, the hero of 'Grease'.

Fax 'n' Figgers

— ABOUT A WORLD STAR

IN THE first film John Travolta ever appeared in, he spoke only seven words! The film was a horror movie called 'Devil's Rain' and in it John was disguised so as to be unrecognisable. The words he spoke were "Blasphemer! Get him, he is a blasphemer". He then melted into a pool of liquid!

ASK MOST people if 'Grease' was Olivia Newton-John's first film and they would say yes, but they would be wrong. Some years ago, she appeared in a film called 'Tomorrow' playing the girl singer of the group with the same name as the film. Olivia would rather forget about that film though – it was a big flop.

HOW LONG do you reckon the first footage of film in which John ever appeared lasted? An hour maybe? Ten minutes? No, just a few seconds. It was in a TV commercial for trousers!

WHEN JOHN Travolta agreed to appear at a huge shopping arcade in Shaumburg, Illinois he little realised that he would have to escape afterwards in disguise. 30,000 people showed up and John had to flee from them afterwards dressed as a policeman!

WHEN JOHN was just a small boy, he fancied himself as a bit of a businessman. In the interest of earning himself a spot of pocket money, he set up a bowling alley behind his home using milk bottles for skittles and croquet balls to knock 'em down with.

Friends were charged 20 cents a game with an extra charge for a glass of soda!

LOVE
— AND JOHN TRAVOLTA . . .
he's linked with many girls, but only one woman really mattered

SINCE JOHN Travolta became an international star, his name has been linked with that of almost every eligible showbusiness lady with whom he has ever been seen.

The romance the gossip columnists would have liked most to see was the prospect of love blossoming between John and his co-star in 'Grease', the lovely Australian-born singer, Olivia Newton-John.

The two of them are certainly great friends and John has spent many a weekend relaxing as a guest at Olivia's ranch home, but both of them have always denied that their relationship was anything more than just good friends and the disappointed gossip columnists have finally got around to believing them.

Among others with whom John's name has been linked are Bianca Jagger, just on the strength of one date they had together and American singer Carly Simon.

After he escorted her to the American premier of 'Saturday Night Fever', John was heard to say ruefully: "I suppose I'll read in the morning that she is about to leave her husband James Taylor for me!"

John's friends tend to laugh at the picture painted by the press of John as a man about town out with one glamorous woman after another. They all verify what he himself says – that he is a one-woman man. In his life, he has had a handful of serious relationships, but the one which outshone all the others was his love for actress Diana Hyland.

They starred together in the film 'The Boy In The

Plastic Bubble', in which John played a teenager who has to live in a germ free plastic bubble because he was born without any immunity to fight common ailments. In the film Diana, who was 17 years older than John, played his mother.

Gradually the pair of them fell in love and, although people commented on the difference in their ages, to them it made no difference.

John still looks back on their time together as the happiest days of his life.

The span of those days was, however, tragically short. Before they had even met, Diana had undergone an operation for cancer. At first it seemed as if it had been a complete success, but eventually it returned and she died in John's arms early in 1977 just after work on 'Saturday Night Fever' had begun.

John was heartbroken and says that it was only the work he had to do which got him through the first terrible weeks after Diana died. Since then he has never found a woman to equal her and never entered into another serious relationship, but the gossip mongers continue with their match-making.

★J.T.★ SUPERQUIZ

HERE IT is – the Travolta Superquiz . . . fifty questions about different aspects of John's life story to test your knowledge of the phenomenon of the Seventies.

Write your answers down on a piece of paper, then check them against the list of answers given on page 44. A total score of 40 or more correct answers out of 50 is the mark of a real superfan, between 20 and 40 correct answers earns you a good 'pass' in the Travolta exam, but below 20 you fail as a Travolta expert and must brush up on the facts!

1. When is John's birthday?

2. In what town and state was John born?

3. What is his second Christian name?

4. How many brothers and sisters does John Travolta have?

5. Are John's brothers and sisters all older than him, all younger than him or is he somewhere in the middle in age?

6. John's father's Christian name is Salvatore, but what is he better known as to his friends?

7. Which of John's sisters had a role in 'Saturday Night Fever'?

8. What is the name of the character John plays in the American TV series 'Welcome Back Kotter'?

9. What is the name of the character John plays in 'Saturday Night Fever'?

10. John played the title role in a TV-film about a boy who had no immunity from illness. What was it called?

11. What was John's nickname as a boy?

12. John has acted in both theatre and film versions of one musical. What is it called?

13. What was the name of John's girlfriend who died in 1977?

14. Who played the role of Stephanie in 'Saturday Night Fever'?

15. What is John's religion?

16. Who wrote and sang 'Stayin' Alive'?

17. What group sings 'More Than A Woman' from 'Saturday Night Fever'?

18. Who is John's co-star in the film 'Moment By Moment'?

19. Who did John escort to the American premiere of 'Saturday Night Fever'?

20. What is the name of the character John plays in 'Grease'?

21. Who was offered John's role in 'Grease' before him and turned it down?

22. What are John's gang called in 'Grease'?

23. How tall is John Travolta?

24. What is his weight (in pounds)?

25. Who plays Sandy in 'Grease'?

26. What is the nationality of the girl who plays Sandy in 'Grease'?

27. 'Saturday Night Fever' is based on an article, which appeared in New York magazine. Who wrote it?

28. Who directed 'Saturday Night Fever'?

29. What is John Travolta's birthsign?

30. What did John originally want to be if he should fail as an actor?

31. John Travolta was nominated for a 'best actor' Oscar. For which film?

32. He did not win the Oscar. Who did?

33. John Travolta is contracted to RSO. What does RSO stand for?

34. How many songs did John Travolta sing in 'Saturday Night Fever'?

35. How many songs does he sing *alone* in 'Grease'?

36. Two songs from 'Grease', on which John Travolta duetted with Olivia Newton-John were British singles chartbusting hits. Name them.

37. What was the name of the disco used for shooting the disco scenes in 'Saturday Night Fever'?

38. Which classical composer had his work updated for a track from 'Saturday Night Fever'?

39. Who will co-star with John in the proposed film 'Fancy Hardware'?

40. What was the name of the vocal group with whom John's mother sang in the 1930s?

41. Which was the first musical in which John ever appeared in the theatre?

42. John's physical fitness trainer for 'Saturday Night Fever' had previously helped another Italian American star prepare for a film. Who was the star and what was the film?

43. How long did it take the Bee Gees to write their songs for 'Saturday Night Fever'?

44. What role does John's sister play in 'Grease'?

45. Which American rock group played Johnny Casino and The Gamblers in 'Grease'?

46. Where is John in the film 'Grease' when he is singing 'Sandy'?

47. What was John's mother's Christian name?

48. What is the name of John's gang in 'Saturday Night Fever'?

49. What happens to Bobby C in 'Saturday Night Fever'?

50. Who was John's stand-in in 'Saturday Night Fever'?

THE "OTHER" TRAVOLTA

– THE MAN WHO STANDS-IN FOR JOHN (AND SOMETIMES FOOLS THE FANS)

It may come as a surprise to some people to know that the hips and legs you see swinging along the street at the beginning of 'Saturday Night Fever' don't belong to John Travolta – they belong to a guy named Jeff Zinn.

Jeff's job in 'Saturday Night Fever' was to be stand-in for John Travolta, which largely means just what it suggests. When shots were being lit prior to actual filming, Jeff would stand in the place where John was going to be, so that the lighting men could make sure that the lights would be exactly right when John came on set to act the scene.

But Jeff also had the job of standing-in for John when his face was not in the shot. For instance, if you see John's arm reaching into a shot to pick up a drink, the arm more likely than not is Jeff's and not John's.

The job of a stand-in is to take some of the pressure off the star of the film by being in position while lights are being set up and by replacing the star for any scenes of the film where the stars own face is not needed.

But for Jeff there was an additional role. Sometimes so many fans would turn up on location that filming became held up because of them. Then Jeff would get up in all John's gear and rush off with fans in pursuit thinking he was John Travolta himself. By using Jeff as a decoy, the set could be cleared long enough for filming to proceed.

Eventually, the fans who followed the film crew around on location got to know Jeff and many of them asked for his autograph. Slightly tongue-in-cheek, he would sign and beside his autograph write: 'To be saved in case of stardom!'

HOW 'FEVER' WAS MADE

B efore 'Saturday Night Fever' was ready for that famous first day of shooting, director John Badham had come to an important decision about the way the film was to be made.

He calculated that if he wanted the story to be realistic, he would have to go, the more expensive route of location shooting, instead of trying to create the scenes in a studio. A key figure on the set became the specially appointed location director, responsible only to the producer and director, and he found himself one of the busiest men there.

As Badham set about the vital task of making his 'family' of actors feel at ease with each other and the film, his location director was scouting around making the final arrangements at sites dotted all over busy New York.

Apart from actually deciding that a particular location was suitable, all sorts of details had to be arranged. Crowds had to be kept at bay, even before the actors arrived – one headache not associated with the studio production.

Anything unscheduled happening in the background had to be removed. A pedestrian crossing the road in the top right hand corner of the screen has to be rehearsed almost as thoroughly as the action up-front: cars belonging to residents of the area have to be found a new parking space during the shooting of a scene.

Most residents around a chosen location welcome the excitement and glamour of a visiting film crew but there are always a few who resent the intrusion.

In this case, the conscientious location director will want to put them at ease, meet as many of them as he can, and generally assure them that the shooting might well be fun after all.

Even things like checking water and toilet facilities, and where the nearest restaurants and cafes are, fall within the location director's province. Filming outdoors also meant that the crew was at the mercy of the weather. Rain doesn't stop – even for John Travolta!

The climax of the film on the bridge corresponded with the most difficult but fulfilling location choice – right on Verrazano Bridge. If the actors had to tread carefully on the bridge, as Tony Manero pleads with his friends, the rest of the crew on the other side of the cameras and lights wouldn't have wanted to jog the huge platform which had been erected beyond the shot for their equipment.

In the event, 'Saturday Night Fever' used over 50 locations, and actors and technicians alike on the film are agreed that its truly authentic street flavour played its own small part in making the film such an undreamed of sensation.

Watch Out For...

John Travolta's film 'Moment By Moment' in which he stars with Lily Tomlin. This movie shows a completely different side of John Travolta's talent with him playing a role far removed from the kind he had portrayed in 'Saturday Night Fever' and 'Grease'.

INFORMATION ABOUT another film proposition. It is hotly tipped that John Travolta is to star in a film opposite his favourite singer Barbra Streisand. The title is 'Fancy Hardware'. Keep an eye out for any bulletins about it.

SUPERQUIZ
ANSWERS

1. 18th February 1954
2. Englewood, New Jersey
3. Joseph
4. Five (two brothers, three sisters)
5. All older
6. Sam
7. Ann
8. Vinnie Barbarino
9. Tony Manero
10. 'The Boy In The Plastic Bubble'
11. Bone
12. 'Grease'
13. Diana Hyland
14. Karen Gorney
15. Scientology
16. The Bee Gees
17. Tavares
18. Lily Tomlin
19. Carly Simon
20. Danny Zuko
21. Henry Winkler ('The Fonz')
22. The T-Birds
23. Six feet
24. About 170 pounds
25. Olivia Newton-John
26. Australian
27. Nik Cohn
28. John Badham
29. Aquarius
30. A pilot
31. 'Saturday Night Fever'
32. Richard Dreyfuss
33. Robert Stigwood Organisation
34. None
35. Two
36. 'You're The One That I Want' and 'Summer Nights'
37. 2001 Odyssey
38. Beethoven
39. Barbra Streisand
40. The Sunshine Sisters
41. Bye Bye Birdie
42. Sylvester Stallone, 'Rocky'
43. A fortnight
44. A waitress
45. 'Sha-Na-Na'
46. At a drive-in movie
47. Helen
48. The Faces
49. He jumped off a bridge into the sea.
50. Jeff Zinn